DEVELOPING EFFECTIVE NEGOTIATION SKILLS

THE FIRST STEPS IN NEGOTIATING

In the business world, skilled negotiation can be the difference between growth and failure. Effective negotiators develop a set of tools and the skills to guide them through their use in the negotiation process. In this course you'll learn how to prepare for negotiations and the skills necessary to communicate effectively for success. You'll also learn best practices for countering ineffective negotiation techniques and overcoming negotiation challenges.

PREPARING TO NEGOTIATE

In the workplace, negotiation is a critical skill. Smart negotiators understand the power of preparation, and have developed a number of specific skills for using in approaching negotiations. The aim of negotiating is to get what you want from the other party. And the best negotiators know that to get what you want you need to focus on interests, not positions. But what's the difference? Well your position is what you want, and your interest is why you want it. When you focus on interests, it's easier to figure out what your counterpart's motivations are.

Even if their motivations are different from yours, by keeping the focus on interests the negotiation can lead to options and agreements that benefit both sides. To get results, first you need to establish what you actually want to accomplish. Think about why you're negotiating. In general you want to satisfy your needs or solve a problem. And those needs and problems are driven by your interests. Then you need to identify common interests you share with the other party, and leverage them.

Consider a situation where you're negotiating a new commercial lease with the landlord. You've already figured out that one of your common interests is stability. You want a permanent office space and the landlord wants a long term tenant. So leverage that shared interest to your benefit. Importantly while you're negotiating, remember to keep the focus on issues, not on people. By focusing on issues you create the right mindset for successful negotiations. But this only works when you do your homework.

Before you even get to the negotiating table you need to find out who you're dealing with. As you build a profile of your counterpart think about their personality. Are they analytical, social, egotistical? You want to tailor your approach to their way of thinking. Really listen to your counterpart, and be prepared to adapt to their style. Successful negotiation requires paying attention to the other side. Don't project your own deficiencies, problems, or apprehensions on to the other party.

Really listen to what the other side has to say, not what you think they are saying or worse what you think they are about to say. It's a common, but often fatal mistake. Recognize that the other side's interests are legitimate too. Don't imply that their interests are unimportant even if you think they are. Show them that you understand their needs and concerns, and that their interests are part of the issue that you want to solve. Show them that resolution can be mutually beneficial.

Negotiating is not about playing the other person or being played. It is not about being tough. It is about focusing on the issues by identifying your own interests. But also understanding what drives the other party by listening carefully to what they are saying. It is about being prepared and being open.

COMMUNICATING EFFECTIVELY WHEN NEGOTIATING

Successful negotiation is a result of effective communication. Well-honed listening, questioning, and speaking skills give you an edge in negotiations. They provide insight into what the other side is thinking and give you the chance to sway the outcome in your favor. The best negotiators are good listeners. Watch that you don't talk too much and listen carefully. By listening more than talking you learn a great deal about the other side. Admittedly listening is hard work. You can become so preoccupied with planning your next argument during negotiation that you forget to listen to what your counterpart is saying.

But by listening well even to those who love their own voices or who try to bully you or waffle about what they want, you can uncover information and attitudes to use to your advantage when tailoring your approach. Good listeners know how to show an interest and an understanding of the other side's arguments and positions even if it is the opposite of their own. A good way to show that you are listening is to repeat phrases in a nice way that the speaker use to summarize their viewpoint.

Show engagement by using phrases like I understand, or yes that's clear to me. Repeat the problem or issue before responding. Taking care to use slightly different wording to show your counterpart you understand. Remember too that asking the right questions is part of effective communication. Ask the kinds of questions that encourage the other side to work with you, not against you. Probing open-ended questions are a powerful negotiation tool for coaxing further information from your counterpart about their interests, needs, and motivation. These questions typically start with why, how, or what, and require more involved answers than simply a yes or a no response.

Conversely while you want the other person to keep talking, don't fear silence. You don't have to speak continuously. Be comfortable with the occasional pause. Only a clumsy negotiator tries to fill in silence. It is especially important if one party claims to have made their last offer and then follows with silence. When this happens the first person to break the silence invariably concedes. You've listened carefully. Ask the right questions. And now it's your turn to speak. Use what you've learned and speak with confidence. Sometimes adopting the other party's rhythm and tone, just a little bit can help establish rapport. Speak slowly and clearly.

When you slow things down both of you have time to think and observe. Be polite and professional but not overly ingratiating. Being too friendly can be off-putting in a negotiation setting. Ultimately the best way of establishing the trust and respect that underlies all successful negotiation is to listen, ask, and speak directly and professionally.

BEST PRACTICES FOR NEGOTIATING

Heading into a negotiation requires advanced preparation. First you must understand clearly what you want to communicate, by using your listening skills, asking the right questions, and speaking directly. Then you're ready to apply some best practices that will enhance any negotiation situation you may find yourself in. Start your negotiation by clearly stating your interest rather than taking a position. Imagine you're buying a new software package for your company. You've identified a great supplier.

The only problem you know your accounting department isn't going to approve the asking price. When you sit down with a rep be direct and state your interest clearly. Say you like the product and that you want to sign the deal. Don't try to manipulate the discussion by pretending you don't want it. When the other party feels that you're being direct the chances are better that when you express your pricing concern, they will be more inclined to negotiate an agreement. While the negotiation process is developing make use of the best practice of remaining open and positive.

Be flexible. People rarely get everything they want out of a negotiation. The process requires both parties to compromise. By being open and positive, you allow the flexibility you need to keep the discussion moving forward to an agreeable conclusion. What happens though if the other side takes a non-compromising stance on an issue, consider the best practice of acting as a moderator rather than reacting as an opponent. Help the other party to understand your stance issue by speaking in a way that shows them that they're not acting in their own best interest.

Say for instance I understand that you value your product and you believe the price is justified. But I can't make a deal at that number. Can I suggest a different approach? By using I phrases rather than you phrases you keep the negotiation open to more flexible options. If you simply said you're charging too much or you're backing me into a corner, you put your counterpart on the defensive. And the negotiation could stall right there. Finally, one of the best ways to keep a negotiation moving forward is offering the other side decision options.

Suppose you ask your supervisor to let you attend a week-long conference. He says he can't spare you for that long. He needs you to facilitate a meeting he is holding that week. Give your boss options that meet both your goals. Tell him attending the conference will help you stay current in your field, but that you'll train a co-worker to help facilitate his meeting. By providing options, you've achieved your own goal while helping your boss reach his. Applying best practices to negotiations ensures you are using the right tools to achieve the best outcomes.

INEFFECTIVE NEGOTIATING TECHNIQUES

Master negotiators do not work miracles. They simply apply best practices they've learned. Smart negotiators know the outcome of negotiation rests heavily on using the right techniques, and staying away from ineffective approaches. Many people get trapped into seeing only two methods of approaching a negotiation, a tough approach or a soft approach. People often picture negotiation as a battle of wills where you need to adopt a tough approach. For tough negotiators negotiation is like stepping into a war zone where you have to use all your weapons to win.

People following this approach insist that all their demands be met. They use a thought process of I'm not giving in. If you want to keep my business you better sign the contract. But following this approach reduces the likelihood of any agreement being reached. When negotiations become a contest of wills finding solutions becomes even harder, and increases that likelihood that the negotiation will break down altogether. Taking a tough approach carries a high risk factor. Some people consider the risk of tough negotiation too high so they take a soft approach.

Soft negotiators are willing to sacrifice results for agreement. The focus is on preserving relationships with the other side and hoping it will somehow lead to the results they want. They want to protect themselves from tricks and manipulation by avoiding conflict and seeking safe, comfortable ground. Good negotiators know that neither of these approaches works well. The notion that either side or both have to engage in manipulation to be successful is risky. It undermines trust and good faith.

And tricks and manipulation are almost always detected by the other party. Another ineffective negotiation technique is sticking to a position without giving much ground. The more you defend and try to convince the other side of the merit of your position, the more committed you become to it. You may also become so committed that you associate your ego with your position. It may feel satisfying to stick to your guns, but what happens then. You lose focus because now you have to save face too. Sticking to a position without flexibility can lead to an unsatisfactory agreement or to no agreement at all. Haggling is another ineffective technique.

Two parties scuffling for an advantage is not a negotiation. Haggling boils down to both sides demanding concessions from the other until both walk away angry and dissatisfied. It doesn't work. Haggling diminishes both sides. Negotiation, whether it's with your boss, a customer, or a business partner should be a collaborative exercise to get the results you want. By staying clear of ineffective techniques, you will walk away with a better result that will make you happy.

OVERCOMING NEGOTIATION CHALLENGES

Manipulation and dirty tricks hinder balanced successful negotiation. And when you are faced with unfair demands in a business exchange it is important that you don't resort to these tactics yourself. Let's say you work for a company that assembles computer hard drives. You're responsible for managing the delivery schedule. You depend on a number of third-party delivery firms. A manager of your biggest delivery partner wants to renegotiate her payment terms. How do you prepare? Start by finding out from your own management what outcome is acceptable. They tell you that you can settle for a 10% increase.

When you meet the delivery manager she demands a 25% increase. How did she arrive at that figure? She says that her own costs have gone up by more than that. You know that isn't so, and you say so. She responds saying that you're inexperienced and that your company has been milking her for the last year. Not true either, but you're not fazed. You're prepared. Take things slowly. Wait until you can make eye contact before responding. You know she's projecting. She's trying to take advantage of your company. Don't accuse.

You want to appeal to her sense of self. You don't want to engage her in a childish and pointless loop of no, I'm not, yes you are accusations. You want to get back to the issues, not dwell on personalities. Don't respond to taunts of personal insults. Instead steer the conversation back to the main issue. Don't allow yourself to be the victim. Now suppose she stonewalls, 20%, she says. That's my final offer, take it or leave it. What do you do? Be the person who can wait. Don't be afraid of silence.

The first person to break the silence usually concedes or walks away. And you know she doesn't want to walk away. Chances are she'll either concede or come down to a figure acceptable to you. You've overcome her negative approach with a successful strategy. You've avoided using any tricks yourself. You've diffused her manipulation and personal attacks. And you've kept her at the table when the discussion could easily have broken down. There will also be times when you have no choice but to seek an alternative that isn't your ideal outcome. Perhaps your counterpart is more powerful than you and you have no choice but to agree.

In those instances you need to seek the best achievable alternative. You set a clear limit by asking yourself at the outset of the negotiation what can I accept. And if your counterpart refuses to negotiate you may need to switch the focus from the subject of negotiation to the form of the negotiation itself. You may need to consider walking away and rethinking your relationship with your counterpart. This kind of drastic action is extreme and rarely necessary. But even then and whatever the negotiation scenario, remember to be prepared. Be open and be positive.

EXERCISE: NEGOTIATING EFFECTIVELY

In this exercise, you'll need to know which methods to use to negotiate effectively with planning, patience, and understanding. In this exercise, you'll demonstrate that you can
- identify effective and ineffective techniques for a successful negotiation
- recognize the effect of different communication practices
- apply recommended practices for negotiating, and
- respond effectively to tricks or challenges from the counterpart

Question

You've decided to approach your manager to ask about working from home two days a week. You know she prefers employees to work at the office.

How might you prepare for the inevitable negotiation?

Options:
1. Outline several personal and professional reasons for wanting to work from home
2. Research advantages for the company of your working from home
3. Plan to question your manager about what her biggest concerns are
4. Prepare yourself by rehearsing counterattacks to any possible objections

5. Prepare a list for your manager of companies that allow their employees to work from home

Answer

Option 1: *This option is correct. One vital step in the negotiation process is to check your own mindset, and to clarify exactly what it is you want to accomplish from the negotiation.*

Option 2: *This option is correct. Looking into the benefits for the company of working from home is one way that you might identify your counterpart's interests.*

Option 3: *This option is correct. When planning for negotiation, you must recognize that the other party may have legitimate interests and concerns which you need to listen to.*

Option 4: *This option is incorrect. This approach views negotiation as a battlefield. You may not be able to understand your manager's point of view, and could end up focusing too much on maintaining a strong position, blocking any progress in your negotiation.*

Option 5: *This option is incorrect. In this case, you're taking a tough approach and trying to manipulate your manager into accepting your proposal, a technique that can easily be detected and may backfire.*

Question

You're negotiating an increased fee with a client. What are the benefits of applying these examples of issue-focused techniques during the negotiation?

Match each technique to its consequence.

Options:

A. You paraphrase concerns that the client has about the fee
B. You ask questions about your counterpart
C. You are not afraid to let a long silence develop
D. You listen attentively to what your counterpart is saying
E. You adopt the client's tone, pace, and style

Targets:

1. Shows that you're interested in their arguments and want to understand
2. Reveals information that you can use in future encounters to

DEVELOPING EFFECTIVE NEGOTIATION SKILLS

show interest
3. Makes you look more in control and stops you from making hasty concessions
4. Reveals aspects of the other party's interests, enabling you to change your techniques
5. Creates rapport between the two parties

Answer

Paraphrasing your counterpart's points is an effective way of building rapport and demonstrating your interest.

Asking questions to get to know your counterpart gives you knowledge you might use to solidify your connection in the future.

By allowing a pause to grow, you can prompt others to make their real feelings or motivations known.

Listening is a vital component of any negotiation as it helps you discover and speak to your counterpart's concerns.

When done appropriately, matching the other person's body language and tone of voice can help build a sense of rapport.

Question

You're negotiating adding a mobile aspect to your customer relationship program with a team leader. She says her team doesn't have the expertise to implement it.

What statements or actions can you use?

Options:
1. Say "I really want the mobile aspect to be included. Otherwise we won't be in the same league as our competitors."
2. Say "I'd like to have everyone on board, so you're either with me or against me on this."
3. Ask her if she has a workaround for the CRM software's mobile access functionality.
4. Say "You're looking at this from the wrong point of view. You need to think about what the competitors are doing."
5. Suggest that they hire a contractor with expertise in that area to help with the development.

Answer

Option 1: *This option is correct. This statement makes it very clear from the outset what your main interest is, and shows her that you're being upfront with her.*

Option 2: *This option is incorrect. The language used in this example is very negative and confrontational. Not only does it create a false dilemma, but it also prevents the negotiation from moving forward. Act as a moderator, not an opponent.*

Option 3: *This option is correct. Asking her for her opinion shows that you're open-minded and flexible to new ideas or strategies.*

Option 4: *This option is incorrect. Using "you" language frequently in your negotiation can come across as accusatory. In this case, it would be better to use "I" language that expresses your motivations clearly and without reproach.*

Option 5: *This option is correct. In this example, you're presenting a possible decision option, which effectively sustains the negotiation.*

Question

What are some ineffective techniques for a successful negotiation?

Options:

1. Insist that all your demands are met
2. Be willing to sacrifice results in favor of preserving relationships
3. Stick to a position without giving much ground
4. Prepare to make concessions until the other party concedes
5. Make your interests known by being direct
6. Remain flexible throughout the negotiation process

Answer

Option 1: *This option is correct. For tough negotiators, negotiation is like stepping onto a battlefield where you have to use all weapons to win. Tough negotiation is all about results. But following this approach reduces the likelihood of any agreement being reached.*

Option 2: *This option is correct. Soft negotiators are willing to sacrifice results for agreement. The focus is on preserving relationships with the other side and hoping that will lead to the results they want. They want to protect themselves from tricks and manipulation by avoiding* conflict and seeking safe, comfortable ground.

Option 3: This option is correct. Sticking to a position without flexibility can lead to an unsatisfactory agreement or no agreement at all.

Option 4: This option is correct. Haggling is an ineffective negotiation technique. Two parties scrabbling for an advantage is not a negotiation.

Option 5: This option is incorrect. Making your interests known from the start is an effective technique to enhance any negotiation situation.

Option 6: This option is incorrect. By being open and positive, you can be flexible in your position when you need to and keep the discussion moving forward.

Question

You ask your boss for a wage increase. She agrees to increase it slightly, but it's below your expectations.

What should you do in this situation to get the negotiation moving forward?

Options:

1. Wait until she makes eye contact again and calmly tell her that you feel the salary still doesn't reflect your level of experience, according to your own benchmarking research
2. Propose that you could also discuss possible performance bonuses in addition to the salary raise that she has offered
3. Inform her of the salary expectation that you had in mind and advise her that you'll accept nothing below that figure
4. Tell her she's mistaken and let her know that other companies would be willing to pay the average industrial wage for your level of experience

Answer

Option 1: This option is correct. By making eye contact, speaking slowly, and staying on the issue at hand, you are keeping the negotiation going.

Option 2: This option is correct. Switching the focus of the conversation from salary to bonuses helps to give the negotiation the fresh perspective it needs to overcome the potential impasse.

Option 3: This option is incorrect. In this case, you are taking a strong position that leaves both of you entrenched in the negotiation. What you need is an intervention that changes the focus of the negotiation and to find another way of connecting with her.

Option 4: This option is incorrect. Even if you feel the other party is mistaken, it's unwise to say so, as they may take it as an accusation. This will only cause your boss to put her defenses up even further. A better technique may be to say that you've reviewed average wages and reached a different conclusion, and then try to get the negotiation back on track.

NEGOTIATING THE BEST SOLUTION

Effective negotiators achieve their goals by reaching agreement. Your negotiating skills make the difference between success and failure. In this course you learn the importance of building and maintaining trust in negotiations. You'll be introduced to personality types, and how to handle emotions and interests during a negotiation. You'll also learn how to facilitate agreement by providing options and how to handle continued resistance. Finally, you'll learn how to close the negotiation.

BUILDING AND MAINTAINING TRUST IN A NEGOTIATION

The key to successful negotiation is forming a relationship with your counterpart. And like any other relationship it needs trust to work. Think of trust as an equation, credibility times intimacy divided by risk equals trust. *[(Credibility * Intimacy) / Risk = Trust]* As credibility or intimacy increases so does trust. But if the risk to your counterpart increases, confidence and trust decrease. A maximum of one hundred points is assigned to each element in the equation. A trust rating above 70 is good, and anything below 50 is poor. Imagine you're working for a large software company. You want to negotiate a deal for the sale of a new product to one of your biggest customers. It's an established customer. So the trust should be high, right? Well intimacy is high thanks to your company's long relationship with them say an 80. But suppose the last time they bought your products, they encountered significant quality issues with the product. This lowers your credibility, call it a 10. They likely consider your new products will have quality issues as well. So the risk is high, 90.

Do the math and the trust rating is only nine points out of 100. *[(10 * 80) / 90]* It's not good at all. How can you build trust in this situation? Your options are to either increase intimacy or credibility or to decrease risk. Your intimacy level is already high. So ask some questions about their quality concerns. If they feel you're really listening to them it will increase your credibility.

You say you've put a more rigorous quality control and assurance process in place, these increase your credibility to 50.

How do you decrease risk? Going forward your company agrees to partially compensate the organization for any costs associated with quality problems caused by the product. This decreases risk to say 50. So by increasing credibility, and reducing risk, the rating has increased to 80. *[(50 * 80) / 50]* This simple formula can help you design a good approach. Your strategy for increasing trust depends on whether you know your counterpart or whether you're meeting them for the first time. If you know someone, you can increase intimacy by appealing to their emotions. Say you're negotiating a pay rise with a tough boss.

Appeal to his sense of nostalgia. Make him remember what it was like for him to secure his footing when he started his first job. Suppose you need to increase your credibility because you haven't fulfilled a commitment in the past. Take the opportunity to explain why that happened and how you're better prepared now. To decrease the risk lay out your plan to meet commitments and include consequences if you don't meet them. If you don't know your counterpart you can increase intimacy by establishing common ground.

Maybe you come from the same town or you support the same sport team. Perhaps you know someone who can provide a connection between you and your counterpart. These can go a long way toward increasing intimacy and establishing trust. If that person can vouch for you, your company, and your track record then it's even better. Even a stranger with credibility like a celebrity endorsing a product or an expert in a field can work. No matter who you're negotiating with, a successful outcome is more likely if you're able to establish trust.

NEGOTIATOR PROFILES

When negotiating, recognizing the type of person you're dealing with is a good step toward tailoring your approach to ensure success. There are four general negotiation personality types. The general, the analyst, the helper, and the sunshine. No one fits a type precisely but most people can be categorized to some degree into one of these four. Have you ever been in a negotiation where you felt threatened? Chances are you've come across a cool and collected general. Their actions serve to underline their importance, and to emphasize that they are the ones in control. They can be quite intimidating.

And that's the idea. They look you in the eye intently hoping you'll flinch and look away. They shake your hand just a little too hard. They speak with the voice of authority and a tone implying that further discussion is unnecessary. The general is all about the results they're after. And what's in it for them, be it increased performance, efficiency, or profit. When you're dealing with a general appeal to their ego. Reinforce their sense of power. For example if the discussion isn't moving forward ask the general to make a decision. Let them feel they're leading.

If the other person is more interested in facts and figures than in resolving the issue you may have a neat, tidy, and polished analyst. They often seem distracted or distant, and their body language reveals little. Much of the time they seem too involved in calculating the endless possible consequences of what's just been said. Because analysts are motivated by facts, figures, logical thinking, and evidence you'll do well to draw attention to your numbers and details. Appeal to their ego. It's of great importance to them as they generally believe they're right. Next is the helper. They're generally warm-hearted, friendly, and cordial.

Helpers remain calm regardless of the situation. They speak in low, hushed tones. They approach issues with a safety-first mindset and seem hesitant at times. To appeal to a helper, speak slowly and remain calm. Make it clear that you feel like they're doing the right thing, and avoid high-pressure tactics. Offer solutions without bulldozing them into submission. Have you ever dealt with someone more interested in the ski reports than in the financial reports? That's the sunshine type with their sunny and open disposition. Some people might live to work but they don't.

They're work-hard, play-hard types, enthusiastic and easygoing. They take great pleasure in celebrating success. Their main objective is to have a good time and experience new things. For them business is just a means to an end. If your counterpart is a sunshine type, then know that wining and dining might be a good method of negotiation. When negotiating, recognize the true colors of your counterparts. And adapting your approach sets the stage for your success.

HANDLING EMOTIONS AND INTERESTS IN A NEGOTIATION

In negotiations, you're always trying to achieve a specific outcome, a certain price, a level of profit, or more resources. Emotions can run high. Anger, frustration, and fear are never far from the negotiating table. Effective negotiators spot and manage these emotions as they emerge. Say you manage a mobile app development company. You've been partnering with a local 3-D graphics company since you started. A larger graphic design company approaches you and offers you the same service but for 25% less.

You have a great relationship with your current partner, and want to stick with them. But given the recent offer you want to renegotiate your contract with them to get a 15% reduction. You explain the situation to him but he immediately gets upset. He points out that he recently lost another contract and that he had to let two people go. He can't give you a 15% cut. He says go with the other company. I'll find someone who's willing to pay a fair price for my service. He's not hiding his emotions.

In fact he's letting them to get the better of him. You could just walk away but you don't want to lose the partnership. So how should you respond? It's best to acknowledge his emotions in an appropriate way. Let him know that you understand how he's feeling but explain that suggesting you go with the other company is a rash decision that's not necessarily in his best interest.

Perhaps this just makes him angrier. He tells you that you have no idea where he's coming from. What now? Allow him to let off steam and get it out of his system.

Don't react emotionally or try to defend yourself. At this point he probably doesn't care about rationales and explanations. Something else you can do is to use the other party's interests to anticipate their next move. You know he's already lost a contract. So even though he said it he knows that he doesn't really want you to take your business elsewhere. So speak to him, emphasize how reaching a deal is in his best interest, and will help him accept the deal. If he's still resisting, try to reach a compromise. Depending on how badly you want to stick with this company you could compromise and meet him halfway.

For example with a reduction of 12.5%, you need a solid approach to manage your own emotions. Avoid knee-jerk reactions. Try to remain calm and stay focused on the issues, not the personalities, emotions, or positions. Acknowledge positive emotions, but don't get caught up in them. You don't want to get sentimental or give the impression that you and your counterpart are too close. That can take you in the wrong direction and lead to feelings of betrayal. Recognizing the existence and role of emotions in the negotiation process allows you to manage them, and reach an agreement in your favor.

FACILITATING AGREEMENT BY PROVIDING OPTIONS

For a strong negotiation with a better likelihood of agreement, it's best to work out a range of options. You have your solution in mind. But chances are it's not the same one the other party is envisioning. After all this is a negotiation. Keeping your options open helps facilitate an agreement. One way to come up with multiple options is by brainstorming with your counterpart. Why? For one, it lets you find as many solutions as possible in a safe space with no judgment. It also helps to develop suggestions that the other party can agree to more easily.

Brainstorming will also clarify the parameters of what you can settle for in the agreement. Brainstorming with the other side increases your chances of getting agreement on at least one of your solutions. A second tactic for facilitating an agreement is finding an appropriate precedent. Nothing is more convincing than a precedent. Say you want to apply for a project management position in a different department within your company. You know that the other candidates from outside your company have better credentials and more experience.

To find a precedent you do your research and look for trends that will help make your point stronger. Talk to other project managers, and examine the projects they've led. You discover a trend. Projects managed by candidates appointed internally tend to be managed better across functionally than those managed by people hired from outside the company. And be direct. Use the knowledge you have gained to offer a solution that benefits you and your counterpart. Get to the point and offer a solution that is beneficial to you and the company.

See something like I have a great track record here working across functions. I may not be the most experienced person you interview but I have great relationships in every functional department. And I know how to work effectively with each one. Then drop the hammer and explain how precedent shows that if you're hired, the chances of a successful project are better. A final approach is to modify a solution to reach an agreement. Let's say you own a start-up that has developed a suite of apps. You approach a major software company to do a distribution deal, but they're not interested in all your products.

How can you generate options? Consider breaking the deal into parts. You may be able to offer individual parts of your product to make the deal more attractive. If there are other parties involved in the deal for example an existing contract with a smaller distributor, you can reduce the number of parties in the agreement or sometimes it may help to make a deal bigger by bringing another party in, say someone who can supply financing. Look for multiple solutions and keep your options open. It will help you get to an agreement faster with goodwill and positive relations intact.

HANDLING CONTINUED RESISTANCE

Negotiating can be slow-moving and confrontational. When you feel like you're waiting through mud, you need strategies to apply to gain agreement in the face of continued resistance. Start by looking at the problem from an external expert's perspective. This requires research and imagination. The key is to step outside your own interests and get an objective view. For example, negotiating a business contract, think of options that a banker might. Maybe you know someone with the right expertise to give you their view or ask someone with specialized mediation experience.

Armed with an external view you can push your counterpart to share this new perspective. Hopefully both of you will see a solution where previously there was only disagreement. You can also adjust the parameters of a solution. Think of a control dial. When you turn the dial toward a harder message, use a softer tone. And if you turn the dial toward a softer message, use a harder tone. Avoid using a soft message with a soft tone which is too lax or a hard tone with a hard message which is too forceful.

Suppose you are a union rep negotiating with management about overtime pay, the talks drag on for days but remain locked in stalemate. Management won't give in on the overtime demands. And workers won't stay past 5:00 P.M. Management turns the dial harder with a soft tone by saying, look, we're not filling orders. We can keep talking but only if you give us 10 hours of overtime per week, then you turn the dial, coming back with a soft message in a hard tone, you say we'll keep all back orders filled if you agree in principle that we'll get an overtime increase.

Other hard options include final, binding or unconditional agreements or agreements that are durable or global. Softer options include partial or conditional agreements, non-binding agreements or agreements on procedures. A similar strategy is switching between the general and the specific. Here you switch from just providing information using broad statements to stating specific consequences. For example there's no way we're going to finish on time but if you give me two more people, we will be okay. Finally another strategy that generates more options and gives parties room to maneuver is single text negotiating.

In this approach create a single document capturing the interests of both sides. The document is typically controlled by a mediator or a moderator. The moderator moves the draft document from one side to the other for successive adding, subtracting, and refining the text. The revision should be flexible to keep the process going. The document becomes a placeholder agreement. Following this approach helps parties shift their focus from grievance to interest. Of course sometimes you'll exhaust all possibilities and solutions, and still not have an agreement. In extreme cases you may need to shut down the negotiation and just walk away. But that's where most situations will yield to a well-played strategy.

CLOSING THE NEGOTIATION

You're almost there. You've reached an agreement with the other party on terms you both can accept. You both believe you're benefiting from the solution you have agreed to, but you're not out of the woods yet. You still need to ensure that you take the right steps with the right timing to close the deal. Before closing the deal you must ensure that you're 100% clear on the agreement. With many negotiations the devil is in the details. Let's say you meet with your boss and reach a broad agreement for a promotion.

You get a 10% raise, an increased bonus rate, and you have a few extra responsibilities. Before getting the paperwork done however you realize your boss hasn't been clear when the raise will take effect, how your bonus structure will work or what your new title will be. She wants to get the documents to HR right away. What do you do? Never forget that more often than not the details are too important to brush aside. Don't let yourself be rushed into making a hasty decision even if your counterpart is pushing hard.

A good tactic in situations where you aren't totally clear on the agreement is to get the advice of a third party such as a partner or a co-worker. Use this to push your boss for further detail. I really need to talk this over with my partner first. So if we could be clear about the timing and the bonus, once you've reached full agreement shake hands and leave. This may seem counter-intuitive or even rude. But sticking around after you've secured a favorable agreement is a bad idea. Many people feel clumsy or even guilty about the situation.

You've put each other through the wringer. Now it's time to make up and be friends. When this happens you run the risk of trying to soothe hurt feelings by talking yourself or your counterpart out of the deal. For example say a union rep just closed a deal to get his workers a significant pay raise. The last thing he should do is tell management how much the workers love the company. Chances are management felt there was a benefit to them accepting the deal, but that doesn't mean they are happy about it. Perhaps they felt coerced or that they've settled for the lesser of two evils.

Any bitterness remaining will only be made worse with a comment like that. Remember your counterpart isn't automatically your friend just because you reached agreement. Always remain professional and keep the prospect of repeat business in mind. Life and business go on. Smile, shake hands and be on your way. There will be many more negotiations to come.

EXERCISE: REACHING A NEGOTIATED AGREEMENT

In this exercise, you'll demonstrate your understanding of critical strategies for securing agreement in negotiations by accepting and integrating your counterpart's emotions, motivations, and unique personality.

In this exercise, you'll demonstrate that you can
- recognize negotiating personalities
- handle emotions in negotiations
- identify and get agreement on options in a negotiation, and
- close a negotiation effectively

Question

Match each example of a way to increase the level of trust your negotiating counterpart has in you to the trust element it can impact.

Options:
1. Lay out a plan to meet commitments, and include consequences for if you don't meet them
2. Ask a third party to vouch for you, your company, and your track record
3. Look for something you have in common with the other person

Targets:
1. Decrease risk
2. Increase credibility

3. Increase intimacy

Answer

You can decrease risk by providing assurances and guarantees about commitments and consequences. You can also decrease risk simply by increasing intimacy and credibility.

A third party is particularly powerful if it's someone your counterpart knows and trusts and someone whose ear you have. But it can also be a stranger with credibility or a celebrity.

If you don't know your counterpart, you can increase intimacy by establishing what you have in common. This will help them feel that you aren't so far apart.

Question

You deal with different personality types when you negotiate. Match each negotiation style with its negotiation personality type. Personality types may have more than one match.

Options:
1. Noel is controlled and deliberate; he asks in monotone for documentation
2. Jean is hard working and lively, with an eye to the weekend; she enjoys new experiences
3. Stephanie is well dressed and distant, a real stickler for detail
4. Tyrone is reserved and cool; he wants results, not discussion, and likes to "stare you down"
5. Julio is quiet and cautious, and likes to take things step by step

Targets:
1. The General
2. The Analyst
3. The Helper
4. The Sunshine

Answer

Tyrone is a General. This personality type engages in power plays, is demanding and focused on results, and is motivated by efficiency and performance.

Noel and Stephanie are Analysts. This personality type is most motivated by facts, logic, and evidence. Analysts are impressed more by accuracy and precision than anything else. They may seem distant and unanimated.

Julio is a Helper. This personality type is most motivated by safety and security. They are cautious in negotiation. Sometimes, maintaining a hushed tone of voice, Helpers will do their best for you, so long as it's the "right thing to do."

Jean is a Sunshine personality. This personality type is interested in having a good time and building relationships. Sunshine personalities are open to trying out new things and like to be relaxed and easygoing in negotiations.

Question

A coworker reacts angrily, saying you're bullying him into helping your team when he's in the middle of another project.

What are the appropriate strategies to use in this emotional situation?

Options:

1. Allow him to finish what he has to say without interrupting him
2. State firmly and with vigor that he is being unfair towards you
3. State that you completely understand the pressures he is under and his feeling bullied by your request
4. Offer his team some support and sensitively; ask if this would perhaps make him feel less pressured
5. Explain calmly and rationally, using evidence, how you are not bulldozing him, and use facts and figures to show him how helping you would be to his benefit

Answer

Option 1: *This option is correct. It may be that he just needs to let off some steam. Afford him the chance to do this before continuing.*

Option 2: *This option is incorrect. Avoid knee-jerk reactions and don't repay strong emotion with strong emotion, or anger with anger. Be aware of and manage your own emotions.*

Option 3: *This option is correct. Acknowledging emotions in a way that lets him know you understand will immediately work to your benefit and keep him on your side. Work with, not against, your counterpart's emotions, and keep your own in check.*
Option 4: *This option is correct. If he's busy with a project you can help with, then this may give you a way back into the negotiation.*
Option 5: *This option is incorrect. Rationales and explanations won't help, because he just won't care. He's too annoyed. Instead, acknowledge his point of view.*

Question
Which tactics can you use to generate multiple options to facilitate agreement?
Options:
1. Brainstorm a solution with your counterpart 2. Find a precedent
3. Be direct
4. Offer a solution that's beneficial for all parties 5. Modify a solution to reach an agreement
6. Insist that all your demands are met
7. Maintain a professional politeness
Answer
Option 1: *This option is correct. One way to generate multiple options is by brainstorming with your counterpart. It allows for creative generation of as many solutions as possible in a safe space with no judgment.*
Option 2: *This option is correct. Nothing is more convincing than a precedent. Do some research. Try to discover trends that will help you make your points stronger.*
Option 3: *This option is correct. Be direct, forthright, and creative when you offer a solution.* ***Option 4:*** *This option is correct. By offering solutions that are mutually beneficial, you can*
change the other party's perspective on the problem.
Option 5: *This option is correct. Slicing the deal into parts, reducing the parties involved in the deal, or making the deal bigger by bringing in another player can all generate more options.*

Option 6: This option is incorrect. This tactic will reduce the likelihood of any agreement being reached. Your counterpart will not appreciate your unwillingness to compromise.

Option 7: This option is incorrect. While it's good to be polite, it will not generate more options to facilitate an agreement.

Question

You're negotiating with a taxi company to improve their telecommunications by providing them with a wireless dispatcher. Which techniques can you use to counter their resistance?

Options:

1. Contrast their more traditional business and the rapidly growing sector of taxi businesses that exploit Wi-Fi and mobile apps to generate business.
2. Use a soft tone when discussing difficult options your counterpart will be uncomfortable with and a harder tone for proposals you think will appeal to him.
3. Widen the frame of your discussions by bringing in someone else from your company to talk with your client about the obvious benefits of Wi-Fi communication.
4. Give your counterpart until the end of the day to accept your proposal or make a counteroffer. Tell him you're prepared to walk away from the whole deal.
5. Work up a placeholder agreement that could serve as the basis of a final agreement. Ask your counterpart to add to, subtract from, or refine the document.

Answer

Option 1: This is a correct option. Switching from the specific to the general – from the taxi company's experience to wider trends in the industry – is a good way to create room for the other party to maneuver.

Option 2: This is a correct option. Hard and soft options add opportunities for flexibility. When you're delivering a harder message, you should always use a softer tone, and vice versa.

Option 3: This is an incorrect option. It is helpful to look at a problem from the point of view of an external expert, but using someone from within your company does nothing to help achieve the kind of objective view that might lead to an agreement.

Option 4: This is an incorrect option. Don't try to bluff or threaten a counterpart into a deal. There are times when you may need to shut down the negotiation, but this should only be done when you've exhausted all possibilities, not simply as a bluff to persuade your counterpart to sign a bad deal.

Option 5: This is a correct option. This technique, known as single-text negotiating, captures the interests of both sides and is controlled by a facilitator or mediator. Revisions tend to be flexible as both parties want to keep the process going. The advantage of this model is that it encourages recognition of mutual benefits.

Question
When dealing with a client, what's the best step you can take to ensure that you have some time to clarify your understanding of an agreement?

Options:
1. Refuse to sign the deal until after both parties have reflected properly to confirm that the agreed proposals match their understanding and intention. At that point, both parties can meet again to accept or reject the deal.
2. Shake hands on the deal. It's taken too much time and effort to reach any kind of agreement to risk unraveling it before it's even signed. Once the deal is made, you will have plenty of time to parse it carefully. You can always try to renegotiate if some part is unfavorable.
3. Inform your negotiating partner that you are obliged to bring the deal back to your management for sign off. Use this step to get your counterpart to supply a detailed description of what they believe they are signing up to.

Answer
Option 1: This is an incorrect option. It is right to take some time to clarify a deal before signing. But by failing to offer a reassuring reason for a delay, this approach risks casting a negative light on the

proposals. Remember, your negotiating partner may already have some reservations.

Option 2: *This is an incorrect option. A good negotiator never makes an on-the-spot decision, unless the situation is totally clear or the stakes are low. A fast decision is rarely a well-thought-through decision.*

Option 3: *This is the correct option. It's a good idea to seek to install a second party to consult with, and to use this opportunity to get your negotiating counterpart to precisely describe the deal's terms.*

www.ingramcontent.com/pod-product-compliance
Lightning Source LLC
Chambersburg PA
CBHW070904220526
45466CB00005B/2126